Live Your Potential and

LET YOUR FAITH
SLEAD YOU TO S
SUCCESS

JOANN YOUNGBLOOD KING

BALBOA.
PRESS

A DIVISION OF HAY HOUSE

Balboa Press books may be ordered through booksellers or by contacting:

Balboa Press
A Division of Hay House
1663 Liberty Drive
Bloomington, IN 47403
www.balboapress.com
1 (877) 407-4847

Because of the dynamic nature of the Internet, any web addresses or links contained in this book may have changed since publication and may no longer be valid. The views expressed in this work are solely those of the author and do not necessarily reflect the views of the publisher, and the publisher hereby disclaims any responsibility for them.

The author of this book does not dispense medical advice or prescribe the use of any technique as a form of treatment for physical, emotional, or medical problems without the advice of a physician, either directly or indirectly. The intent of the author is only to offer information of a general nature to help you in your quest for emotional and spiritual well-being. In the event you use any of the information in this book for yourself, which is your constitutional right, the author and the publisher assume no responsibility for your actions.

Any people depicted in stock imagery provided by Thinkstock are models, and such images are being used for illustrative purposes only.
Certain stock imagery © Thinkstock.

Print information available on the last page.

ISBN: 978-1-5043-2902-6 (sc)
ISBN: 978-1-5043-2903-3 (hc)
ISBN: 978-1-5043-2904-0 (e)

Library of Congress Control Number: 2015903437

Balboa Press rev. date: 03/20/2015

This book is lovingly dedicated to
My mother, Bettye Youngblood

CONTENTS

ACKNOWLEDGEMENTS

I would like to thank and acknowledge my Success Glam Squad for their continued support and encouragement: Niya Allen, Kevin Dunn, Maria Enaboifo, Kimani Harvey, Crystal Jones, Bradley Lowary.

I cannot express enough thanks to my assistant Electra Ford and coach Marcy Nelson-Garrison for their help to hold me accountable and keep me focused on my goals and dreams.

My sincere gratitude and appreciation to my mentors: Daisaku Ikeda, Les Brown, Iyanla Vanzant, Louise Hay, Oprah Winfrey, Wayne Dyer and Joe Vitale. Thank you for being a wonderful example for me to follow and giving me the motivation and information I need to help others have happy and successful lives.

My completion of this project could not have been accomplished without the support of SGI-USA, Project

Enterprise, my family, friends and associates. I truly appreciate all of you!

And, lastly a special thanks to my son, Julian for offering a quote for this book. I love you!

FOREWORD

By Greg S. Reid

A few years ago when I was browsing the Web for inspiration, I came across a unique blog by Lew Rockwill, president of the Mises Institute which promotes Austrian economics.

The title caught my attention because as an entrepreneur I was struggling to make some decisions. It said simply: "The Faith of Entrepreneurs."

"There are thousands of reasons why entrepreneurship should never take place but only one good one for why it does," Rockwill wrote.

"These individuals have superior speculative judgment and are willing to take the leap of faith that is required to test their speculation against the facts of an uncertain future.

"And yet it is this leap of faith that drives forward our standards of living and improves life for millions and billions of people. We are surrounded by faith. Growing economies are infused with it."

As an author, speaker, filmmaker and entrepreneur myself, it made me think about this other characteristic of success of which so little had been written: the concept of needing faith to develop ourselves and achieve our personal best success.

When Certified Success Coach JoAnn Youngblood King contacted me to write the foreword for her latest book, *Live Your Potential and Let Your Faith Lead You to Success*, I was pleased to oblige for two reasons.

The first is that I am a fan of the passionate approach JoAnn has for her life-coaching. I enjoy reading her blogs and articles and have been personally inspired by them.

The second is that I believed a thoughtful exploration of the link between faith and developing our full potential was essential literature for those of us who coach others to achieve their best lives.

JoAnn makes the claim that I have come to accept from my own personal experience as valid.

She writes: "Faith is the single biggest force available to propel you to your best work and your best life."

This book is a wonderful journey to a new way to consider personal development in a world that for too long has focused on aggression, taking advantage of people and situations, and looking after number one as a road to success.

Cynicism and selfishness are not workable building blocks for your personal development. Cynicism isn't playing it smart; it's playing it scared. You are afraid to trust in anything to work out, afraid to trust others to do their best work with you, and afraid of yourself to climb mountains for views the rest of the world hasn't yet seen.

Selfishness may advance your cause and allow you to soar over a few obstacles, but when you do trip and fall, and ultimately you will because you are human, you will not be able to call on anything bigger than yourself to get up again. Self becomes very small and inadequate under such circumstances.

JoAnn's book about faith and success is a wonderful guide for those of us who want to live our lives unreservedly and achieve success. From the hundreds of motivational speeches I have delivered in recent years, I am aware that people seek inspiration more than anything else.

They have a dream, and with that dream, they have doubts. They want to let go of their security blankets and slip into a whole new world of achieving their dream, but they can't find the strength to make the big decision.

If they could reach for faith, either from somewhere in the great beyond or within themselves, they would find something strong enough to hang onto and something flexible enough to launch them under any circumstances.

In my personal life, I have known what it is to reach for faith to move myself to the next level of achievement, and how heart-warming it is to win the faith of others. A recent expression of that was when I was selected by The Napoleon Hill Foundation to help carry on this great man's teachings. As I was writing *Think and Grow Rich "Stickability": The Power of Perseverance*, there were many moments when I had to have faith that I could do the job.

Self-doubt would have long ago destroyed most of us if we didn't have trust in somebody or something, despite our lack of logical proof. And that is the definition JoAnn uses for faith.

We believe that we can start a successful business. We believe that if we can capture an idea with words or art, that people will read it or look at it and be inspired themselves. We believe that we can grow our talents and flourish as individuals as long as we keep the faith.

Live Your Potential and Let Your Faith Lead You to Success is a book you need to read when you are just charting your course in life; it is a book to read when you reach a milestone and are trying to decide which road to take. I would also suggest it is a book to read when you are thinking about retiring from your regular work and turning your energy and time into creating something that you have always wanted but abandoned for the unselfish reasons of feeding your family with a steady paycheck.

Regardless of what stage you are at in your personal development, you will be able to take a valuable message to heart to kick start another phase of your life.

What is particularly useful, besides the message of this book, is the way each chapter ends with ideas for personal reflection and then some ideas for action.

We cannot grow without taking time to think and sometimes coaches forget that. I love that JoAnn has made that a priority throughout the book, which gives it a beautiful interactive quality.

Because of it, readers will feel like they are making the journey to faith and success together with this gifted author.

Bestselling author and acclaimed speaker Greg S. Reid is an entrepreneur known for his giving spirit and special skill of translating complicated situations into easy-to-understand concepts. Published in more than 45 books, 28 bestsellers, and five motion pictures and featured in countless magazines, his special gift is his ability to guide strategy into results. He stresses the importance of relationships and character in his writings as he guides his students to success.

INTRODUCTION

Faith is a word many people won't use when they speak about their plan to build a successful career and live a fulfilling life.

They are afraid it will make them look weak or passive: a "turn-the-other-cheek" kind of person who will never have the courage or fortitude to climb the success ladder.

The connotation of the word "faith" has changed throughout the years. Instead of being a standard to live by, there is a whole category of people who consider faith to be a characteristic unconnected to a logical thinking process.

They think faith is something that can close our minds to what is real and keep us from seeing, understanding and reacting wisely to the world we live in.

It isn't.

Every day that I work as a Certified Success Coach, I realize more acutely that it is actually the opposite.

Faith is the single biggest force available to propel you to your best work and your best life.

I define faith as your belief or trust in somebody or something despite your lack of logical proof.

It has been my experience that having faith changes you in the most positive ways you can imagine.

It pries open your mind and lets in the light of fresh thinking. It sweeps away your worries, clears out your fears, and leaves you free to create your best self.

It is also a logical process, one that you may have embraced as a child and then abandoned as an adult because you could not bring yourself to buy into what you could not explain.

Faith will give you the courage to live unreservedly and to achieve success beyond your most fanciful dreams. It will fuel your passion and ignite your vision. It will fill you with calmness and chase away the destructive force of negativity.

In the ten chapters that follow, I invite you to join me on a journey of discovering faith and letting it into your life to help you grow.

In this book we will study faith from the perspective of:

- How it can inspire your actions
- How it can ease your troubled mind
- How it can help you get the results that you want
- How it will serve to eliminate obstacles and
- How it will help you realize your amazing potential.

We will look at ways we can embrace faith and reflect it in our actions to get the success that we want in our work and in our life. We will use it to hone in on our mission and do the work and make the contributions we want to achieve.

At the end of each chapter we will take time out to reflect on faith in our lives and then take an action fuelled by our faith. Please take the time to do both, for faith without action will not come alive with its full power.

I know that faith is essential in my own life, and I want you to experience its value in yours. I witness the difference it makes daily in my practice as a Certified Success Coach and as a Business Trainer and Facilitator.

You can read the chapters in sequence, or just select them randomly for quick reads during your busy week. Each carries a complete message and a complete coaching session.

I wish you all the best on your journey. When you are finished, send me an email and tell me how it worked for you. I am also available for private coaching sessions.

You can reach me at: JoAnn@liveyourpotential.com.

CHAPTER ONE

How to Develop Your Faith and Yourself

There is a Buddhist term, Honnin-myo which means from this moment on. It expresses the concept that every moment is a new beginning.

No matter what has gone on in your life up to this moment, if you are ready to be successful, now is the time to make a fresh start. This moment, as you start to read this book, is your new beginning.

What you will learn about faith and its power now will help you obliterate those things from your past that are holding you back from having the life of your dreams.

You have the potential inside of you to have the type of life to which you aspire. You may not be aware of that, or be confident of that, or trust that. Your potential may

1

be chained to the cement blocks of your doubts. But it is there, ready to be activated.

To be successful, all you really need is to have the faith to simply get started.

Will mistakes happen? Will obstacles stand in your path?

Possibly.

However, remember that mistakes and obstacles only come to help you grow. It doesn't matter how many times you try something; you can always start over again.

And the time that you have the faith that it will work, it will.

The world is full of people who became amazing success stories because they had the faith in themselves to keep trying.

Nelson Mandela spent most of his life in jail fighting the injustice of the apartheid system. He never stopped fighting and finally saw his goal realized.

Henry Ford went broke five times before he founded the amazingly successful Ford Motor Company.

R. H. Macy, a man who often talked about the impact of faith in his life, had seven failed businesses before he succeeded spectacularly with his store in New York City.

The story of being successful is about having the faith to "start from now" and try again.

Do you have that faith?

This book will guide you to develop it and use it to pull out the goals and dreams inside of you and make them a reality.

The important thing to realize is that you come to this moment primed for success. The ability and the drive is within you; you just haven't extracted it yet.

Believing, trusting and having faith will bring it out and make it happen.

Start from now.

The beginning of the process is developing your faith. The middle is learning how to use that faith to bring out your own personal best to make the essential decisions and life choices that will lead to your success. The happy ending is your achievement of success and your acceptance of it as the way you wish to lead your life.

Let us talk first about the development of your faith.

We are all born with faith. Faith is the belief that the parent who cradles us in their arms will not drop us. It makes us stop crying and snuggle in, feeling warm and safe. Gradually, this sense of trust and faith grows stronger. As a toddler, we will jump into a swimming pool into the arms of our parent or care-giver, trusting they will catch us and keep us from drowning.

Faith is a simple concept when we are young. We believe in those around us and we believe in a force greater than ourselves to guide us.

As an adult, our faith is shaped by our experiences. Even people who proclaim they have no faith actually do have it; they just don't recognize it for what it is.

For instance, one person believes that they will have wonderful eyesight because they eat carrots every day. The fact that they have maintained 20/20 vision all of their life confirms and strengthens their faith in this fact. Because of their experience, they have developed faith in the benefit of eating carrots.

This is a very simple example of how we develop our faith.

When you believe in and trust in something so strongly, it develops into knowing. There is a certain peacefulness and calmness in knowing what you know.

Faith is a very powerful quality, and the single most powerful quality to help you achieve success.

When you grow up and embrace life's disappointments and disillusions, you grow wary of faith. You challenge yourself that faith has no place within your logical thinking.

We need to re-develop our faith if we are to grow and succeed to the best of our potential.

One of the best ways to start doing this is to start again to believe in the goodness of the universe in general and the people whose lives touch ours in particular. We cannot let the bad things that have happened to us destroy our faith in the potential for good things to happen.

Our world is full of natural beauty and rich resources that sustain us. The miracle of sowing seeds to grow our food is a visible expression of our faith in this universe. So is believing that the air we need to breathe will continue to be there for us, that the sun will warm us, and the rain will nourish our fields and help us produce a harvest to sustain us.

It is a graceful transition to move our faith from the universe to the people in it. The more people I meet in my coaching business, the more amazed I become at the goodness and talent most people possess. Getting to know them reaffirms my faith in human nature daily. I have faith that despite the occasional bad things that people do, the bulk of individuals mean no ill to their fellow man and are merely struggling to make the most of their own potential.

Developing faith in our world and its people are the easy parts. Developing faith in yourself is the difficult challenge. It will take a process starting from today that will take you down a road of learning to understand your potential, to control your worry and anxiety, to believe in your capabilities and to find the courage to take the actions to succeed.

I have noticed that people who have strong faith are not easily swayed by any negativity or obstacles that come their way.

This is why having strong faith is so important when striving to have a successful life.

To be truly successful, developing faith is not enough on its own. You must also live your life in a manner that shows proof of your faith. You must let your faith guide your actions.

Having faith without using it to guide your actions is a wasted resource.

You need to act on your faith. You need to let it inspire your actions. What you will discover is that taking these actions is much easier once you have faith. The two are tightly inter-woven.

Faith is associated with believing in and trusting an unseen force in the universe which governs everything. While this force has been called many names by different religions and philosophies, what is constant is that faith is best expressed as part of your own personal experience and connection with that force.

Think about what you believe in. Even on your darkest day, there is someone or somebody or something that still sparks your faith. Cling to that and prepare to summon it on your road to success that lies ahead.

Something to think about:

Fear knocked at the door. Faith answered. And lo, no one was there.

- Anonymous

Faith is daring the soul to go beyond what the eyes can see.

- William Newton Clark

Something to do

Set aside time today to begin a faith journal. Think about the universe around you and write down some things that you believe to be true about it. What parts of your world do you have faith in? Think about your family, your children and your friends and consider your faith in them. Look deeper now, deeper than your world and your close circle of people moving through it. Do you believe in a higher overall power? Can you find a source from which you can be empowered?

Finally, think about yourself. What do you know for sure about yourself and your abilities and potential? What do you have faith in? List these qualities in yourself that you know you can summon as you need them.

Chapter Two

Do Your Actions Reflect Your Faith?

We now know that simply having faith is not enough to succeed.

We need to live our faith by taking actions.

The encouraging aspect of faith is that once you develop it, it will inspire your actions and make them easier to accomplish.

It will also help you pull from yourself the ingredients to succeed.

Living my faith always makes me think about a television commercial I used to see many years ago.

The commercial referred to fresh ingredients that good cooks would use if they were making spaghetti sauce from scratch. The company used the commercial to assure viewers that even if this sauce came packaged in a jar, it was as vital and tasty as one which was made from scratch.

When clients talk to me about what they want to achieve and how they are going to overcome obstacles, I find myself reminding them that just like the fresh ingredients, their potential for success is in them.

Their faith will guide them to the actions they need to take to achieve their goals.

I know from personal experience that through faith you will be able to summon the strength and skill needed to live the life of your dreams.

I am so grateful to have supportive people around me who help me keep my faith and stay focused on my goals and dreams. They keep reminding me when I stumble that the potential is in there and then I find the strength to bring out what I need to overcome whatever struggle I am facing.

I am also able to contrast the difference it makes between having faith and not having it. This is how I would illustrate that.

Many years ago I saw a woman walking down the street with her daughter. Just as they were passing by me, I heard the little girl say: "Mommy, where are we going?"

The woman replied: "Be quiet and just be happy you're going somewhere!"

When I heard this, I thought that this is probably one of the reasons why some people walk about aimlessly, without knowing where they are headed in life, or not even striving to do something that makes their lives better.

When the people we have faith in don't encourage us to understand our destination and reach it, it is difficult for us to trust our own internal compass.

Lack of faith in our abilities from the people close to us also eats away at our faith in ourselves.

When I was about 14 years old, my older brother asked me what I wanted to be when I grew up and I said "I want to be a statistician."

He said: "Oh, you're not going to be able to do that."

I never even questioned why he thought that. I just started thinking of something else I could do.

I'm sure the intention of the little girl's mother and my brother was not to stop us from moving forward with our dreams and goals. However, messages such as these get filed right into our subconscious mind

As children, we may not have had so much control over what we saw or heard growing up. However, as adults, we definitely have control over what we choose to take in.

What you put into your mind has an effect on your whole life. It impacts your perspective on things and your faith in the world around you, and ultimately, your faith in yourself.

Watching the news can often cause you to worry and keep you in a constant state of fear. Also, being around certain people can keep you in a negative frame of mind.

If you find yourself in the presence of anything that may not be helping to move you to a higher level of success, do what you can to remove yourself.

I'm not suggesting that you stop watching the news altogether and I am aware that you may not be able to avoid some naysayers. I'm simply saying to be mindful of how you are choosing to react to or hold on to the information you are receiving.

Faith is fuelled by positivity. That is not limited to just your efforts to speak positively about life, about others, and about yourself. It is equally important for you to seek out positive and uplifting messages and let them into your mind on a regular basis.

One reason I've been able to accomplish many goals is my consistent desire to look for the positive in life. I listen to lectures and read voraciously all the literature about self-improvement and being a success. I know that to a large extent what goes into our minds is what comes out.

I have a second reason for exuding positivity. Because of the nature of the business I chose, as a success coach I want to be fuelled with positivity and be able to apply those positive messages to help others achieve success. Helping others to succeed is my passion.

Positive messages touch your soul and elevate your spirit. They make you smile, infuse you with energy, and spur you to take action to achieve success.

Focusing on and seeking out positive messages will also make it easier for you to view in a better way any obstacles that may arise. For example, I'm sure there have been times in your life when you were told "no," perhaps from a potential client. Hearing the word "no," doesn't mean never, it just simply means "no."

For that client, at that time, they were not interested. For every person not interested in what you have to offer, there is someone who is interested. There are millions of messages, so make sure you are listening to and applying the positive ones.

It is important to listen to all the messages and sort through what you believe.

You can only do that when you have a firm grasp on what you do believe.

What do you stand for?

Knowing what faith and beliefs are deep inside of you help people to better grasp who you are and decide if they want to help you or not. Always remember, it's not what you say, it's how you live your life that speaks volumes.

There are many people who try to convince others to do what they say or to believe what they believe. It's important for you to know that the real way to convince someone of something is to show them with your actions.

Your actions really, really do speak louder than your words. Take a look at your faith and ask yourself: Am I showing proof of my faith through my daily actions?

Think about all the spiritual, business and political leaders of the world who announce what they believe in and then, by their actions, destroy all of their own credibility.

Think of others who inspire us for decades by putting into action the faith they talk about. Those are the people you believe.

As an entrepreneur, you may decide to find a mentor to help you achieve the successful life you desire.

Would you rather have a mentor who tells you what you should do or a mentor who shows you with his or her own life how you can accomplish your goals?

It would be in your best interest to find someone who is walking the talk instead of just talking the talk.

I've heard parents say to their children: "Do what I say, not what I do."

Regardless of that request, most of the time children end up doing what their parents do instead of listening to what they say to do.

If you find yourself complaining about the way someone else is living their life, instead of complaining, focus on you. Make sure that you are doing your best to be a good example. Don't talk about it, be about it.

Being a great example to others is one of the greatest gifts you can give them and exemplifies what it is like to live with faith.

Be the example of your faith. Be the example of your values. Be the example of what you would like to see in others. You can make a bigger impact on the lives of others when you lead by example.

Something to think about:

Faith is a bird that feels dawn breaking and sings while it is still dark.

- Rabindranath Tagore

Faith does not make things easy – it makes them possible.

- Anonymous

Something to do:

From this moment, start taking action towards your dreams and goals. Make two fresh new action steps this week towards your success.

There are people in need of the services you offer. Think about how your actions and how you present yourself will help to convince them you are the real deal, that you live the faith you have in yourself and them.

In your faith journal, start to experiment with writing advertisements and presentations to present yourself and your product as a true reflection of what you are about.

Summon the faith you have within yourself to engage your potential. Take the step you have been thinking about for a long time but lacked the faith to start. You can do it! Just get started.

CHAPTER THREE

HOW TO TELL IF YOUR PRAYERS ARE BEING ANSWERED

I was speaking recently with a client who was going through a really rough time.

She said: "I've been praying and praying and nothing is happening. I don't know what I'm going to do."

I have heard those words many times before.

In fact, when I was a child, I viewed prayer as just a means of asking for stuff that I wanted, as in "dear God, please bring me an easy bake oven like Carleen's for Christmas."

If I got it, my faith was renewed. If I didn't, I felt like my client, wondering if anyone was listening."

Neither myself as a child, nor my client as an adult, really grasped the concept of prayer.

Prayer is defined as a sincere request to God or an object of worship. I respect it as a practice that has been part of our culture and traditions almost from the start of time. My perspective on prayer has changed a lot over the years.

Prayer is indeed asking for something, whether it is guidance, relief from a worry or an illness, or a general plea for help to overcome what life has sent our way. But it is only the first step. There is a second, very crucial step that must follow if we are to know if our prayers are being answered (and they will be).

I now understand that praying is important, but what we do after we pray is even more important.

As adults, we pray primarily because we are worried about something. We fear that we won't be able to care for our families because we have lost our jobs. We fear we won't be able to fulfil our responsibilities because we have been diagnosed with an illness. We fear for our business during tough times, for our children when they are skirting the edge of trouble, and for ourselves when we can't find answers to our problems.

So we pray, and as soon as we stop praying, we start to worry again.

We forget to initiate the follow-up to prayer.

The follow-up is quite simple.

Once we have finished praying, we need to summon our faith and believe that the answers to our prayers will come. We do not need to know exactly when or how they will arrive. We just need to remind ourselves, over and over if necessary, that we have prayed and answers will come.

Correspondingly, we must banish the worry and leave our minds open, willing and able to receive the answers when they arrive. Author Sharon Lechter is quoted as saying "To worry is to pray for what you do not want."

A mind clouded with anger, fear, distrust, worry and uncertainty cannot possibly let the answers in. How can we even hear with all that noise in our heads?

Instead, we must empty these negative thoughts from our heads and use our faith to stay strong with an open mind while we await the answers. Faith is absolutely necessary to having your prayers answered.

Consider, for example, that you have prayed because you are worried that your business will fail. I suggest that you pray, have faith and then take action.

An interesting thing happens after you pray.

What you focus on in faith expands.

So if you are focused on your business succeeding and your faith is strong, you can be confident that your prayers will be answered.

You will naturally just keep taking action towards success. You may not even understand that your prayer is being answered until much later when it is apparent that the action that you took after prayer was precisely what you needed to do.

This interrelation between prayer, faith and action is unfailing. Because of it, you can do whatever you set your mind to do.

This concept has become very evident to me when I worked with several clients in recent years that have lost their jobs in a difficult economy.

Those who have faith and pray, and those who do not, fall into two distinct categories.

Those who lack faith in themselves and believe their prayers are not being answered are upset, depressed and constantly complaining about their troubles. They talk to anyone who will listen and agree with them about times being hard and how there are no jobs and money available.

The second type are optimistic and happy about the new opportunities ahead of them. They have chosen not to take in what the media and others are saying about the economy and are focusing on the positive.

Many of them have prayed for new jobs and found them. Many have prayed for guidance to take a new step in their lives and they have started successful businesses.

I want you to be very clear about the message I'm conveying to you. Yes, it is true that there are problems and issues in life we must face. However, your success is determined by how you take in, process and handle those problems and issues.

When you have faith in the world, in a higher being, or in yourself, it manifests itself as power to win back your own life.

Did you know that you have the answers to the questions you seek? Do you know how powerful you are? Do you know that you can accomplish any goal you choose to? Do you know that whatever problem you are faced with right now, you can figure out a way to solve it?

If you are not doing, being and having all that you want, you must take a look at what you are feeding your mind.

Be constantly aware of what you are thinking about and focusing on, in order to keep moving to the level of success you aspire to. Focus on your success.

As Norman Vincent Peale said: "Formulate and stamp indelibly on your mind a mental picture of yourself as succeeding. Hold this picture tenaciously. Never permit it to fade. Your mind will seek to develop the picture."

Your faith will move you to take the right steps. Allow room for your vision to spread by moving the clutter of negative thoughts. New ideas that will lead you to success will rush in to fill the void and lead you to your full potential.

Something to think about:

Sometimes you have to stop worrying, wondering, and doubting. Have faith that things will work out, maybe not how you planned, but just how it's meant to be.
- Anonymous

Faith consists in believing when it is beyond the power of reason to believe.
- Voltaire

Something to do:

In your faith journal, write down one thing that is sorely troubling your mind. Consider all the aspects of this problem, why it upsets you, why you can't solve it, and what will happen if it is not solved.

They pray about it.

When you finish praying, rid your mind of all the negative thoughts about this problem. Just think about the problem itself and know that within you there is the power to solve it.

Let a few hours, perhaps even a night pass without worrying about it.

Think about it again and consider an action to solve it.

Take that action. Your faith will guide you in the right direction.

CHAPTER FOUR

HOW TO ERADICATE WORRY FROM YOUR LIFE

Many of my clients confide in me that they are really worried about one thing or another.

I define worry as being uneasy in our mind, feeling anxious about something. The dictionary adds that it means to fret, to pull at or tear at something.

To me, worry is a member of the fear family.

As with fear, most worry is not based on any reality about what is happening to us or what will happen to us.

Most of the time we worry about something that has not or will not happen. But we think it will.

It is part of our human nature that worry will enter our minds many times in the course of the day. When we crawl into bed at night, it moves to the top of our minds and demands attention, a plague of the darkness.

Since we can't absolutely eradicate it, why don't we change the way we deal with it?

Did you know that the word "worry" also means to advance or manage despite trials and difficulties? We "worry" a thread through a needle, for example. Another description of worry is to move with effort.

Isn't that interesting?

It puts a much more positive light on worry. In fact, viewed that way, perhaps worry isn't such a negative force after all.

When you find yourself worrying, summon your faith and remind yourself that even though you may have to employ some extra effort, you will manage to get through the current situation. After that, you will advance again, regardless of how rough the immediate challenge you are facing is.

If you feel that your worrying is overwhelming and you still feel uneasy or anxious, the other antidote is trust. Have faith in yourself that you will weather the storm.

Attack your worrying habit the same as you would attack any other characteristic that you wanted to eliminate from your makeup. Start by analyzing what it is you worry about. Is what you think you are worried about (a particular challenge) really what is bothering you, or is it just a small piece of a larger puzzle.

Remind yourself that worry is not a static state. Worry means that you will work something through, even if it takes a little more time and effort than you anticipated.

Trust yourself and know that you can get through whatever it is you are worried about.

Sometimes it is helpful to go right up to the worry wall in your mind and ask yourself what would happen to you if what you are worried about actually happened.

Suppose you have heard that there are layoffs coming in your workplace and you are really worried that you will be affected. If it happens, what will you do? Will you look for another job? What other jobs might be available that match your skillset? Is there any additional training that you need to get those new jobs? Is your resume polished and ready to send at a moment's notice?

Sometimes the simple act of making a plan of action eases your worry.

Maybe the job layoff will be the impetus to start your own business. Have you time now to at least get your business plan together and get your company registered?

Can you worry this potential problem through to a logical plan so you are ready to get right back up on your feet if you get knocked down?

You can apply this kind of thinking to any problem. Are you worried about a pending doctor's appointment because you believe you are ill? What will happen if you get a bad diagnosis? Is your health insurance up to date? Have you a support system you can draw on? What kind of medication or treatment is available to help the kind of problem you think you have?

This is not to encourage you to waste your precious time solving problems that don't actually exist, but rather to help you wrestle the worry monster down to a size that you can handle.

Ideally, if you have faith that you can manage what happens to you and that what happens to you is meant to be, then you can eliminate worry from your life. You cannot control everything, and once you accept that, there is very little worth worrying about.

But if you must worry, find a way to do it constructively so you can submerge your worries and focus your creativity and attention on positive actions that will help you reach your full potential.

The successful people I have met, rarely worry. They know that they can do what they want to accomplish. Fuelled by faith in themselves and the skills they have gathered throughout the years, they move ahead confidently, not wasting time on second-guessing themselves.

They are equally unconcerned about what others say about them. Their focus is to move forward, and they are not sidetracked by the darkness of worry or the blur of gossip.

You can be like that: strong and confident. When your faith in yourself is well developed, you will know that between the power within you and the power outside of you, no situation will be more than you can handle.

Then you will be free to focus your efforts on acquiring the success that you desire.

Something to think about:

When the heart weeps for what is lost, the spirit laughs for what it has found.
-   Sufi Aphorism

Every tomorrow has two handles. We can take hold of it by the handle of anxiety, or by the handle of faith.
-   Old English Proverb

Something to do:

In your faith journal, make a list of your biggest recurring worries.

Think about how long you have been plagued by those worries and how few of them have actually happened.

Think about how you would cope with them if they did happen.

Then, having put them on the page and out of your mind, resolve to commit them to a different existence, one that is far removed from your thoughts and your actions.

You have faith; you can do what needs to be done regardless of the challenges ahead. You do not need to slow yourself down and diminish your energy and resources with the burden of worry.

Chapter Five

How to Surrender Your Need to Control

There may be times when you can get caught up worrying and complaining about the obstacles that stop you from accomplishing your goals.

However, complaining and worrying about negative experiences on your road to success is counterproductive. Instead of oiling your progress for a smoother ride, complaint and worry will actually serve like a glue to keep you stuck in one place.

When you find yourself stuck in a negative spot, you have to stop and surrender to your faith.

In our culture, we unfortunately equate the word "surrender" with "defeat," but in reality they are not the same at all.

The spiritual principle of surrender is not about giving up. It is the act of letting go, the acknowledgement of the power of spiritual activity.

It is an understanding that we don't have to consciously do everything ourselves, that our faith will see us through.

Surrender is one of the most important spiritual principles and the most challenging. Practicing surrender helps you to stop worrying, complaining and agonizing over problems or situations.

Have you ever been in a situation where you were held up or stopped from taking an action you wanted, but there was absolutely nothing you could do about it? Perhaps an accident has closed a road and you are tied up for hours in a traffic jam. Perhaps your daily routine has been interrupted by a notice that you must be evacuated from your home office because of a tornado or flood? Perhaps a snowstorm and blizzard-like conditions has knocked out your electric power and you are unable to communicate by phone or Internet with anyone.

Do you get upset and work yourself into a frenzy?

More likely, you will do like most others and realize that you are in a situation that you cannot control, so you must make the best of it and take simple steps to secure your comfort or survival in the midst of this chaos.

If you are tied up in traffic, you use your cell phone to call those who are waiting for you and explain what happened. You snack on food you may have packed in your car. You may read a book or use your time to think about a new business initiative you want to work out.

If you are being evacuated, you pack only those most basic things without which your life would be terribly complicated and you go. You suddenly realize how little your "stuff" means in relation to taking the step to save your life.

If you have lost your ability to chat or the phone or surf on the Internet in a snowstorm, you surrender to what you cannot change and settle down with a good book. You check to see if your alternate sources of heat (like a wood stove) are primed and ready to go if the outage lasts a long time. You go to bed earlier as darkness descends and have faith that power will be restored with the brightness of the next morning.

There are many circumstances that happen to all of us that make us realize we must surrender control and just move forward with the resources available to us.

With faith, we understand that we don't have to wait for a crisis to adapt that kind of behavior.

In our everyday lives, regardless of what is happening around us, things will work out better if we realize we cannot control everything. As soon as we start to relinquish some of that control, our burden is lightened and we become more creative in our solutions.

Part of having faith is accepting that sometimes you just have to pray and then let go of something, realizing that you cannot control the end of every game you play.

Or, to put it another way, even the greatest warrior cannot fight and win in every war.

When you ease up on the control and have faith that problems will ultimately be solved, they suddenly become more bearable. More often than not, problems solve themselves.

This is the principle of surrender to faith, and it is powerful.

Think about surrendering when you realize you have come up against a situation you cannot solve at that moment in time. Let go of the negative thoughts and obstacles that you believe are stopping you from accomplishing your goals.

Remember that you are becoming successful with every action you take toward your goals.

If there is an action that you took that didn't give you the result you were looking for, then that was a lesson learned.

Don't agonize over it. Don't fret. Let it go!

Accept the lesson and keep moving forward.

As innovative thinker, scholar and co-chair of the Deloitte Center for the Edge John Seely Brown writes: "The harder you fight to hold on to specific assumptions, the more likely there's gold in letting go of them."

Having faith means you are confident enough to accept that you can't control everything. From that acceptance comes growth.

Something to think about:

Faith is raising the sail of our little boat until it is caught up in the soft winds above and picks up speed, not from anything within itself, but from the vast resources of the universe around us.
-   W. Ralph Ward

Faith will move mountains.
-   Old English Proverb

Something to do:

Practice surrender. In your faith journal, write about the thoughts or obstacles you believe are stopping you from accomplishing your goals. Then draw lines through them as if they don't exist. What is left is your freedom on the road to success. Have faith that you will get where you want to go even if you don't control every mile of the road to get there.

CHAPTER SIX

HOW TO LEARN THE ART OF TRUST

Stephen M. R. Covey, author and son of success guru Stephen R Covey, has written a new book called *The Speed of Trust.*

In the book, he suggests that trust is the very basis of the new global economy and the essential ingredient for any high-performance, successful organization.

Trust in yourself is also the very basis of developing an attitude of faith that is the essential ingredient for your personal success and the means to achieving your full potential.

There are many definitions to explain trust. Personally, I like to think of it as a confident expression of your faith. But it is also an expression of hope, of integrity, of strength and of ability. It is something we can rely on.

Most of us have a pretty good idea of how to secure the trust of others, but no unearthly idea how to build trust in ourselves.

The two processes are actually very similar.

If you wanted a stranger to trust you, you would show them consideration and kindness, you would be consistent in your actions, you would do things to assist them in helping to achieve what they wanted to do, you would stick with them when times got tough, and you would not betray the faith they would have in you.

If you want to trust yourself, you must also show yourself consideration and kindness, be consistent with your actions, help yourself to achieve your potential, keep the faith during difficult times, and stay true to what you believe in.

When you promise yourself that you are going to change and grow, you must take actions every day to prove to yourself that you have faith to stay the course.

When you encounter difficulties, just as you would not desert another, do not desert yourself and fall into despair or a quitting mode. Stick with yourself because you know that within you is the power to overcome these obstacles and emerge stronger when they pass.

As you stay true to yourself despite all the conflicting ideas that enter your head, your faith in yourself and your self-esteem will rise.

What happens when you start to trust yourself?

You will find it easier to trust others. You will engage in an upward ladder of trust, moving tentatively and then confidently a step at a time.

You will embrace the competence of others and be more understanding that you cannot take on this world and achieve your personal best without the help of others. You will find it easier for your words to match your message.

Perhaps for the first time, you will really know yourself. You will stop gliding through life on autopilot and take a firm grip to steer your life in the direction that will help you achieve your personal successes.

You will become more willing to share your thoughts, your values and your impressions. You will begin to more deeply understand what matters to you, and what you must guard closely and what you can throw away.

In an earlier chapter we talked about eradicating worry as we now know it and learning to trust ourselves. This is a concept we need to explore further, since finding enough trust to have faith in ourselves is much more difficult than having faith in anything or anyone else.

Trust means gaining total confidence in yourself and your ability to become successful.

At its most basic application trust means you can live without being constantly worried about your survival. You trust that you will have food to eat and a safe place to sleep.

You trust that your heart will beat, your blood will flow, your lungs will expand, and that your feet will stay firmly planted on the ground.

You just trust that certain things will be okay, and they are.

What happens if you cannot trust and believe in yourself?

Going through life without faith and trust in yourself and others is painful. If you put up a wall and keep others at bay because you think you are protecting yourself, you are not.

The opposite actually happens. Instead of staying safe you will just stay scared, full of pain and doubt and fear and never living life to the fullest.

We have all experienced the pain of betrayal. That is the dark side of trust. But we cannot let it dominate our lives. It is possible to overcome that disappointment and trust again.

With faith in yourselves and others you can achieve a success and happiness that exceeds your expectations.

Something to think about:

Faith is to believe what you do not see; the reward of this faith is to see what you believe.

- Saint Augustine

Faith isn't faith until it's all you're holding on to.

- Anonymous

Something to do:

In your faith journal, every day this week write down one thing that you want to do. Start with something really, really simple like: I want to clean up the dishes after supper so the counter will be clean when I come out in the morning.

Or, I want to read three pages in a book today. Or I will walk for five minutes.

And then do it.

Change the action every day and every day, note that you have done what you said you were going to do.

Once you have achieved this, do it for two additional weeks. What you are trying to establish is a habit of trust.

It seems inconsequential to write down such small accomplishments and record that they have been done, but it is effective training to help you believe in yourself and know that what you want to do each day, you will achieve.

CHAPTER SEVEN

DO YOU KNOW WHAT YOUR LIFE'S MISSION IS?

Motivational speaker Les Brown said that when he was younger, people would often say in response to someone stating a goal or a dream:

"You have as much chance to do that as people have to walk on the moon.

Who knows what kind of amazing ideas where stopped after hearing that statement? And now we all know how wrong it was.

When I was younger, I just thought of my imagination as something that was not here now, and that's it. I remember hearing comments like: "Oh, that's only in your imagination" or "that's some imagination you have there!"

To me, my imagination was a silly, unrealistic thought. I definitely didn't get the message that what I imagined should be pursued or better yet, could be achieved.

I now know differently.

I know that what any of us imagines is possible with faith. The hardest job we all face, however, is determining what our life mission will be.

Your mission is your role on this planet. The Arizal, 16th century Kabbalistic master, preached that no one has ever or will ever come into this world with the exact same mission as yours.

Your mission is your unique footprint in the sands of time.

Your mission, fuelled by faith, is essentially the role that you want to take in your life. You may want to build buildings or build up people; you may want to help and heal, you may want to teach or touch people with your words or art.

Only you will know when you search your heart what your mission is to be.

And don't stop looking when you determine one mission. You may walk this earth to fulfill several missions. The child you raise may be destined for greatness; the work you yourself do may support a team that makes a difference in how people live. The book you write may thrill your generation and many generations to come.

Do not worry if you have already started a career and a family and haven't yet taken the time to really identify your mission. Lots of people do that because they just don't have the knowledge as they apply for their first or second job to know what they are really seeking to do.

That is because all of our early schooling, followed by our community college or university training, is heavily focused on accruing skills and knowledge, not on understanding ourselves.

As an adult, you enter the labor force and start your role in society much like a carpenter who has been given all the tools and the knowledge to use them, but no plan about what he or she is to build.

Our mission is figuring out what we have to build, what our master plan is.

You may work for many years and still not really grasp what your true mission in life is. Sadly, some people go to their grave still unsure of what their lives meant.

You will know that you have achieved your mission when through your faith in yourself you suddenly feel a sense of joy in what you are doing. When you are excited to do more of it and your mind is racing about all aspects of it, then you know you have found what you were meant to do.

You may feel your mission when you stand in front of a classroom for the first time, or when you read your first x-ray and determine what is wrong with your patient. You may feel it when you cradle your newborn baby in your arms or when you fix your first car. You may feel it more than once, and then you know you have more than one mission.

Once you know what your mission is, your next job is to heighten your faith to believe that you can accomplish it. Then you pray, and you plan, and then you take actions to fulfill your mission.

You may encounter obstacles along the way, but you will find the resources within yourself to surpass them. The faith you have developed will see you through the difficult times and chart your course to success.

When you just can't figure out what step to take next, pray about it, and then take the next action that comes into your mind.

Having faith helps you to understand that you came into this world specially equipped to fulfill your mission, to achieve your own special brand of success.

If you have not yet discovered your life's mission, set aside some quiet time to consider what you really want to do with your life. Believe that it will become clear to you if you open your mind to it.

The beautiful thing about identifying your mission is that it clears your mind and crystallizes your faith. It helps you set a plan to head in your chosen direction and to dismiss all the other distractions that are not taking you where you want to go.

Your faith will be strengthened, because you will feel that your efforts are not validated. You know you are heading down the right track. You have faith that within you are the tools and the talents to accomplish your mission and working on it becomes a joy, not a job.

Imagine what accomplishing your mission and finding true success in your life looks like. Ignite your imagination.

If you are still seeking your mission, take some time to write about the type of life you imagine for yourself.

Just give some thought to how you can start making some of what you wrote down a reality.

Start on a smaller scale. Imagine the type of week you would like or the type of day. Remember, it's possible.

What does being successful mean to you? Everyone has their own definition of success. Some people say that they are successful once they have received their college degree, the dream job they were able to land or a wonderful family life.

All of these definitions certainly contribute to living a successful life.

However, what most of us may not realize is success is not necessarily something to be achieved. Success is something we must allow.

Once you really realize what your mission is, fear disappears. You become more focused and you naturally develop a structure that works.

You are already successful. You are capable of doing anything you desire! It's all up to you!

Something to think about:

If we desire our faith to be strengthened, we should not shrink from opportunities where our faith may be tried, and therefore, through trial, be strengthened.

  - George Mueller

Let your dreams be bigger than your fears, your actions louder than your words, and your faith stronger than your feelings

  - Anonymous

Something to do:

Concentrate on finding your mission in life. In your faith journal this week, write down five things you have done in the past month that gave you great pleasure and a sense of fulfillment. Do any of them have the potential to become a life's mission?

Another exercise in defining your mission is to consider what you would spend your time at if you were so wealthy you didn't have to take a job to make money to live on. How would you spend your money and your time if you had an endless supply of both? The answer will lead you to your mission.

CHAPTER EIGHT

WHAT ARE YOU DOING WITH YOUR POTENTIAL?

Ralph Waldo Emerson said that shallow men believe in luck.

"Strong men believe in cause and effect."

I learned about the Law of Cause and Effect when I was introduced to Buddhism many years ago.

What this law means is that there is a corresponding effect for every cause made.

If you want to know why you are or are not reaching your potential, just look at the causes you have made, or are making, to bring about the results that you are getting.

In order to be successful, happy, or rich, you need to make the causes to get the results you want.

If having your own business is what you desire, start making the causes now to get to that result. Being aware of the Law of Cause and Effect helps to keep you on the right track.

Pay attention to the causes you are making and they will lead you to where you want to go.

Have faith in yourself to understand that you have the potential for great success.

So what are you doing with that potential? Have you made any effort toward living your potential?

Most people want to be successful; they want to be happy and have the freedom to live their lives any way they want to.

However, how many of us actually make the effort necessary to achieve the level of successful we aspire to?

Maybe you need to come up with a different strategy or plan of action. Make some very specific causes towards your dreams and goals.

Realize that you are the one who makes the choice to live the way you do. The potential for success is there! Please don't allow that potential to stay dormant.

Have faith, be positive and take the action necessary to allow your success to emerge.

Take an inventory of your life. Are you living your life the way you want to?

Make a list of your dreams and goals. Write down the steps that will bring them to reality. Map out your strategy to achieve what you want. Then start with one initial action. Follow it with another, and another, and another.

To keep your faith strong, write a couple of affirmations to say every day that will remind you of the great potential you have for success.

Here are five affirmations I use personally to stay focused and positive.

- "I realize that I am the one who makes the choices to live the way I do. Greatness is a choice – I choose to let my greatness shine through!"
- "I choose to be positive and speak positively. I know that being and speaking positive can only benefit me and others."
- "My form of prayer gives me hope and allows me to let go of any worries or concerns I have while I am on the road to fulfilling my dreams."

- "There is one powerful source in the universe that governs everything. I am connected to that source. Through my faith, I trust that I will be provided with everything I need."
- "I know that taking action brings results. I will take consistent action towards my goals until they are accomplished."

IF your road to success is through business, or you are already a small business owner, examine yourself to ensure that you are passionate about what you are doing to grow that business and develop your own potential.

Many entrepreneurs start a business because they believe that particular type of business will be very lucrative, or they simply want to have the status of being a business owner. Sometimes they just don't want to work for someone else.

There is nothing wrong with all of those reasons. However, when you are not really passionate about the business you are in, it may take a long time for it to be as successful as you want it to be. When you don't have faith in it, your actions will not expand to bring in the results that you desire.

Realize what your passion is. It differs from your mission in that passion is what fuels your actions to accomplish your mission.

It's interesting that for those who say they don't know what their passion is, they do have an idea about what it is not. What do you love to do? What would you rather be doing with your time? What brings you joy? Answering questions like these will help you to become aware of your passion.

Also, keep in mind that we are creative. We create with our words, thoughts and actions. It will be helpful to change your language about "finding your passion." Start by acknowledging that you do know what your passion is, because you really do! Create another affirmation or declaration to repeat.

For example, you might tell yourself "I am becoming more aware of my passion every day." Realize that saying you have not "found" your passion is saying that it is somewhere outside of you. It is not. It is still within you, and your faith will release it when you look hard for it.

Something to think about:

Faith is courage; it is creative while despair is always destructive.
- David S. Muzzey

Faith is spiritualized imagination.
- Henry Ward Beecher

Something to do:

Consider all the things that you do in the average day. List them in your faith journal. Of all those things, which actions fill you with joy and ignite your life? Which ones would you miss if you did not do them again?

Do this exercise for five consecutive days. The things you would miss are the clues to what ignites your passion. A clear pattern will emerge.

Chapter Nine

Cultivating the Power of Consistent Effort

One afternoon my son mentioned to me that he didn't want to do a particular homework assignment because it was too hard.

Have you ever expressed some tasks as being hard to do? I certainly have.

I started thinking about that statement and wondered what type of outcome I was looking for when I've said something is hard to do. Was I looking for empathy or was I just giving myself a reason not to complete the task?

By saying that the homework was hard, my son was hoping it would get him out of doing it. I, on the other hand, realized that he just had to do a little extra work in order to get it done. Because it would take a little longer to work on, it would take some time away from his play time afterwards. That was the real issue. It wasn't that the homework was hard, it just took a little more time to figure out.

I have come to realize that it doesn't matter whether a task is hard or not. What matters more than anything is the determination and desire to complete the task at hand and our faith that it can be done.

For example, it may not be an easy task for someone to leave their job and step out on their own to start a business. However, because of their passion, determination and strong desire to succeed, they do it anyway. They move closer to doing the work that helps them fulfill their mission and become successful as a result.

It is important not to let thinking that a particular task is hard prompt you to stop doing it. Only by summoning the faith and talent within you will you complete the task and then move forward, one step closer to fulfilling your dreams and goals.

As we discussed earlier, our attitude about our tasks rests a great deal on our perception. If we see a challenge as a barrier, we can become resentful of it and shy away from what needs to be done. If we see it as an opportunity to take us closer to the success we desire, we are more able to find a solution and put it in place. What you think and the words you speak have a big impact on your life.

Since I'm always striving to speak positively, instead of saying that a task is hard, I say that it is challenging. Saying that the task is challenging helps me to get through it easier.

In order to get rid of any negative thoughts that come up, you have to constantly plant good thoughts in your mind. I created another way to make things easier for myself. Instead of seeing a task as hard, I see it as H.A.R.D., by which I mean Helpful, Adventurous, Rewarding and Dynamic.

When I look at things that way, tasks take on a whole new meaning.

There are many reasons that stop people from achieving their goals. Failure to summon their faith to guide them through the difficult tasks is a major one. Facing one too many challenges has stopped a great deal of people from accomplishing their goals. It has happened to me in the past and I suspect it has happened to you.

With faith, you can get past that and continue on your road to success. No matter how many obstacles you believe are standing in the way of accomplishing your goals, you will know in your heart and soul that it is possible to achieve them.

Your faith will give you the power to practice consistent effort, and consistent effort is the sure and steady way to achieve your success.

First, keep in mind the great potential you have. Second, take little steps every day towards your goal, no matter how small, and third, never give up on your dreams!

Pay attention to the efforts you are making towards your success.

Through the development of your faith, you know without doubt now that you have the potential for great success! What are you doing with that potential? Have you made any effort toward living your potential?

Most people want to be successful; they want to be happy and have the freedom to live their lives any way they want to. However, how many of us actually make the effort necessary to achieve the level of success we desire? Are you consistently working towards your dreams and goals?

I loved math in high school. Trigonometry was my favorite subject. When I had a test coming up, I would make up my own test before the real test. I use to put math formulas up on my bedroom wall to remember them. I also tutored some kids in math in my neighborhood. I joined the math team in school and the friends I hung out with loved math as well. I was very consistent with my love for math. When it came to subjects I wasn't that interested in, I only studied when it was absolutely necessary.

Over the years, I had forgotten about the importance of being consistent until I started studying personal development and realized my mission to help people become successful. I now make an effort every day that contributes to my success and the success of others.

I have come to realize that an important factor in being motivated to make consistent efforts is loving what you do. When you are passionate about your business and how you want to help others, you are motivated to take actions to be successful in your field.

But there is another reason why applying consistent effort is a crucial part of achieving success. That is that consistency builds trust and makes people take notice of you and your product or service.

Babies are consistent when learning how to walk. They don't try walking one day and then decide to try again in another day or two. To them, walking is exciting, it's new and it will get them where they want to go. So they keep working at it consistently until they accomplish their goal.

We must view our efforts to achieve success the same way. Success comes with consistent action. Do at least one thing daily to take you a step closer to your goal. If you have no idea what to do, a good place to start is to began reading about it.

Reading something positive daily will help inspire you to make positive changes in your life.

Something to Think About:

To have great courage you must have great faith.
-   Julian Joseph Haynes

Reason is our soul's left hand, Faith her right.
-   John Donne

Something to do:

I've learned that you have to put in many, many, small efforts that nobody sees or appreciates before you achieve anything worthwhile.

Take out your faith journal and make a list of 10 steps you could take that would bring you much closer to the success that you seek.

Assess the list. Do the things that you feel capable of doing on your own, and seek help for those too large or daunting for you to try alone. There are life coaches like myself on the Internet or in your community to help you. Don't be afraid to seek help to get your success in gear.

CHAPTER TEN

HOW TO GET THE RESULTS THAT YOU WANT

Are you familiar with the poem "A Dream Deferred" by Langston Hughes?

In this poem, he questions what happens to a dream that is put off or not acted on.

Basically, the poem suggests that if no action is taken towards your dreams, you dreams will not happen

What stage would you say you are at regarding your dreams? When you think about the dreams you have, do they seem realistic?

For some people, dreams are something they hope will come true one day, if they are lucky. For some, their dreams are so big that they have no idea how to start taking action towards them.

What are your dreams? Do you have a plan of action toward them or have your dreams been deferred?

It's important for you to go after your dreams. When you are focused on and working consistently towards your dreams, not only will it be easier for you to knock down any obstacle that comes your way, you will also experience tremendous growth and success in your life.

How much effort are you putting into being a success? How do your results look?

The types of results you are getting are equal to the type of effort you are putting in.

I heard about life coaching in the late 1990s and knew immediately that this was something I wanted to do. I already had a passion for helping people to see the potential for greatness they had inside.

I decided to become a success coach and started studying everything I could about it. I made up a name for my coaching business, made up business cards, and started telling people about coaching.

Even though I love everything about coaching, I wasn't putting the kind of effort into my business to get the results I was looking for.

For the first six years of saying I was a success coach, I was seeing no results.

I had fear and doubt about my abilities, no real focus, no structure, and no clients!

It wasn't until I hired a coach myself that I realized what was most important to me as a coach. I wanted to help people to become aware of their potential for success and to take action based on that potential.

I wanted them to get results.

Since starting my coaching company, "Live Your Potential" (www.liveyourpotential.com), I have been able to help many people get the kind of results they are looking for.

No matter what business, product or service you provide, remember that you are doing it for results that will benefit you and others as well.

In order to be successful, you must always keep in mind the type of results you are after.

Take a look at what you are doing right now. If you are not as successful as you want to be, you need to make some changes in your actions.

One of the biggest excuses I hear for why people are not getting any closer to the success they seek is that they do not have time to think about and take the proper actions to make success happen.

It's not that you don't have the time; it's that you don't have the faith to keep on plugging, action by action, to get where you are going.

When you decide to start a business, you will have to make some necessary changes in your life. Maybe you don't like to change. Maybe you have a fear of success. I'm sure there are many possible reasons you could have for not allowing yourself to be successful, however, time should not be one of them.

Make time to succeed. Take inventory of how you are using your time. Find at least 30 minutes a day to do at least one thing towards your dreams and goals.

Consider all the key categories of goals in your life. These might include work, relationships, fun, health, education, finance, community service and spiritual.

Consider which of these categories that are not successful. Then ask yourself how you could do things differently to get a different result in this category.

Ask yourself if you are holding on to misconceptions or old ideas that aren't relevant anymore and if it is time to clean up your mind and open it up to prayer.

Do a cross-check to see if your actions are aligned with your business values. And speaking of values, do your personal values conflict with your business values? You can't get a clear fix on success if they are at cross-purposes.

Revamp your route to success by abandoning actions that drain your energy and upset your calm. You are not meant to operate in that way. You attract what you do, and until you make significant changes, you will continue to be stuck in your old way of plodding through the day, ending no closer to success than when you started.

Ask yourself every day "is this what I really want to do?" If it isn't, you may find it difficult to draw out your best skills and traits to apply to the challenges. If it is, you will set out to do it with a joyful heart and your creativity fuelled for all challenges.

You are totally responsible for what happens in your life. Having the faith to take that responsibility and use it wisely will regenerate you and bring you success. Shirking that responsibility or refusing to meet it head-on will keep you trapped in a kind of working limbo, productive up to a point but never soaring ahead to the warp speed of maximum potential.

Something to think about:

Faith is like electricity. You can't see it, but you can see the light.

- Anonymous

Without faith I can do nothing; with it all things are possible.

- Sir William Osler

Something to do:

Have you developed your faith sufficiently to figure out where you are going and to fuel and direct your actions to get you there?

Practice acts of faith and trust daily to take your quest for fulfillment and success to attainment. You can do it. It's in you!

Know too that while you have everything inside of you to become the success you want to be, you may benefit from professional help to develop your faith and use it more effectively as you discover your mission and the route to achieve it.

Conclusion

If you are serious now about going all the way on your journey to faith as a means of achieving success, I want to assure you that you don't have to do this all alone.

Having a certified life coach to help you make you establish your goals and develop your strategy can be an amazing help to making what you want a reality. I say that not to sell you on the idea, but to be my own humble acknowledgement that I could not have achieved the happiness and success I have accomplished in life without the help of others.

I have benefitted from life coaches in my own life greatly, and in fact, their support in providing me with the tools, the support and the structure needed to achieve my dreams is the reason I recommend that road to you.

I have developed a unique introductory coaching program called "Be the Next Top Success Story" which includes six weeks of success coaching.

The program is straightforward and inherently useful. It is not just platitudes; it is skillful strategy and wisdom to teach you how to tap into your successful self, to recognize your talents and abilities and to capitalize on them right now.

It is designed to help you formulate and take the necessary actions, step by step, to achieve the results you desire.

I will personally coach you and give you all the tips, tools, motivation and encouragement you need to bring out the best in you.

If you are not quite ready to go on the journey to success yet, I understand. Change can be challenging.

But I believe you are ready, because you have taken the time out of your busy life to read this book. Clearly you are seeking answers, and I congratulate you for taking this first, single action to change your life.

If working by phone and over the Internet is more conducive for your schedule, certified life coaches like myself are only an email away.

You can reach me at <u>JoAnn@liveyourpotential.com</u> and I can quickly give you details on various success coaching formats that will fit your lifestyle.

Meanwhile, get out your faith journal and review all the options and actions that you have resolved since you started to read this book. Know that as you make your plan, you will be fuelled by faith to achieve what you set out to do.

ABOUT THE AUTHOR

JoAnn Youngblood King, Certified Success Coach (CTA), is an author and owner of Live Your Potential, a coaching company that has assisted many in achieving personal success in their lives.

JoAnn, who has a diploma in Small Business Management, is a business trainer and facilitator for Project Enterprise, an organization that provides access to business loans, business development services and networking opportunities for entrepreneurs and small business owners.

Her coaching style has been described by her clients as "relaxed and effective."

Coaching is delivered by phone and email.

"JoAnn is extremely passionate about helping others to succeed," says a recent client. "She is dedicated to helping you find your path to success and has great listening skills. She helped to keep me focused and on track to accomplish my goals."

Her motto is: "You have the potential inside for great success. Now is the time to Live Your Potential."

JoAnn has been coaching professionally since 2004.